Play *REAL* Golf
Relaxed • Enduring • Actively • Learned • Golf

K. Tracy Roberts M.S. Ed., PGA
with
Stephen Plummer PGA

dog ear
PUBLISHING

Play *REAL* Golf
Relaxed • Enduring • Actively • Learned • Golf

K. Tracy Roberts M.S. Ed., PGA
with
Stephen Plummer PGA

Contact the authors at PlayREALGolf.com

First published by:
Dog Ear Publishing
4010 W. 86th Street, Ste H
Indianapolis, IN 46268
www.dogearpublishing.net

ISBN: 1-59858-228-3

This book is printed on acid-free paper.
Printed in the United States of America

Foreword

Forget your opponents; always play against par
-Sam Snead

When "Coach" Tracy Roberts asked me to write this Foreword, I was honored and excited. I was honored, because he is such a special person; and excited because the words you are about to read can completely change the way you think about both the game of golf and the game of life.

Most people who play golf believe that if they just had better equipment, a better swing, or better partners, they would have a better game. The fact is, the physical aspects of playing golf are only one part of the game. This book will show you that there are other aspects that you have to focus on as well. As I often say, for things to change, *you* must change.

The truth is, in golf as in life, *you* are your only opponent. By setting a higher standard for yourself and consistently working to exceed that standard, you can experience dramatic change in any area of your life. It's not about competing with someone else; it's about being the very best that you can be at everything you do in your life.

One of the key themes in this book is that positive energy creates positive results. I talk about this in my audio program, *The Burning Desire*. In it, my friend and mentor Joseph McClendon III and I describe how to create that positive energy. We say, "See it, feel it, be it, have it."

Play REAL Golf will teach you to do that with your golf game.

I enjoyed reading this book tremendously, and know you will too. Make sure that you actually complete the exercises in this workbook, though. It's not good enough to just read the information, you have to take action. Writing your answers to these questions is the first step in becoming the golfer you have always dreamed of becoming.

Dare to Dream

Doran Andry

Acknowledgments

Thank you to our families and friends that have contributed to the development of this project.

Jerry, your guidance and loyalty have been phenomenal. Schmitty, your valuable and poignant words of advice have been tremendous. Kevin, your willingness to spread the word is essential for our success. David, your visual imagery has made the project come to life. Doran, your inspiration to "dare to dream" has been the fuel that made this dream a reality. Trevor thanks for "Keeping me REAL". Nobie, John, David, Annette and Sean thank you for keeping it REAL for all these years. To all the other REAL players, thank you for sharing the amazing game of golf.

Thank you to our families for all of their support. Most of all we would like to thank the ladies in our lives, Mary Ann, Samantha, Stefany and Holly. Your patience and support have allowed us to inspire golfers throughout the world.

Apparel provided by: Dockers®
Eyewear provided by: SUNDOG™
Golf Bags provided by: Izzo Golf®
Photography by: Mr. David Zogg

TABLE OF CONTENTS

INTRODUCTION TO THE REAL GOLF PROCESS CH. 1

In this Chapter
- ➤ <u>Performance Elements</u>
- ➤ <u>One Game, Different Bodies</u>
- ➤ <u>State of the Game Address</u>
- ➤ <u>Exercises</u>
    - ⇒ Why Play Golf?
    - ⇒ One Game, Different Bodies
    - ⇒ Playing Your Game

I congratulate you on your decision to truly enjoy the game of golf. Golf is the greatest metaphor to life that sports has to offer. No other sport offers a better opportunity to enjoy competition, camaraderie, and a connection with nature. The honor and dignity of the way the game of golf is played has endured through the ages. People all over the world enjoy playing this game that has such a very rich heritage. The truth is that many people play golf, others play REAL golf.

It seems that more books have been written about golf than any other sport. So a logical question is, "Why *Play REAL golf?*" *Play REAL Golf* will coach you through a process that will build synergy within three essential performance elements. These essential elements are the *psychological,* or for our purposes the *emotional,* the *experiential,* which means the learning that comes *from playing,* and the *kinesthetic* which describes the *physical motions* of the golf swing.

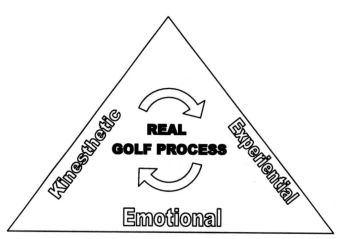

The *REAL* Golf Process integrates the performance elements.

The three performance elements work together. Golf performance is much like everything else that we do in life. Feelings affect our physical being as well as how we evaluate information. To reach our potential as players we must integrate all three elements into the learning process. Establishing a *REAL Golf Process* that combines the emotional, experiential and the kinesthetic performance elements allows players to play their best golf.

Too many players believe that the key to improving one's golf game lies solely on the mechanics of the golf swing. That is they concentrate on the kinesthetic aspects of golf. They take lesson after lesson that work on the mechanics of the golf swing. They learn how to swing a golf club. They also have the latest swing tips given to them by their buddies and can discuss the latest theories put forth by the multitudes of publications regarding the golf swing. Some people fail to improve even though they practice occasionally. Many spend day after day, week after week, working on their swing, yet they never improve their performance on the golf course.

To improve overall golf performance and *Play REAL Golf* all three elements must be addressed. *Play Real Golf* will focus on the area most often overlooked, the emotional and behavioral element, through an interactive process. The *Play REAL Golf process* **can be used effectively with any swing method that you choose.**

Why a workbook? I have been fortunate through the years to work with many mentors. Teachers, coaches, business leaders, as well as personal development experts have all inspired me to write down thoughts. They have all shared that once you write something down you take ownership of those thoughts. Play REAL Golf will coach you through *the REAL Golf process* in a workbook format. To get the most from *Play REAL Golf*, it is important to complete all of the exercises thoroughly and honestly. The writing exercises will allow you to examine your feelings and your game. This will allow you to own *the REAL Golf Process.*

Everyone who plays golf, from the beginner to the PGA Tour player, is on a constant journey to improve. People are constantly looking for the answer to the question, how can I get better? One particular mentor, entrepreneur, motivational speaker and author of several books on personal development, Doran Andry has an answer to that question with a message that rings very true. He is very successful in helping people change their lives, and his message is straightforward. "For things to change you must change." This may seem self-explanatory, but it is very important. Many golfers expect improvement to happen, but they repeat the same self-defeating actions. Much like golf the message is simple, but not easy. Golf is a simple game. Hit a ball into a hole.

Many people want to create change but they find it very difficult. *Play REAL Golf* will provide you with a workable system to create positive emotional-behavioral changes that will improve your performance and more importantly your enjoyment of the amazing game of golf.

Play REAL Golf has been developed based upon almost four decades of combined teaching and coaching experiences. We have introduced golf to those as young as four years old and continued to coach those in their eighties. Some have never touched a club before; others compete at the highest levels. There are a multitude of stories that have come from years of sharing the game of golf.

The first step I take with everyone whom I coach is to talk with them about their life and about golf. I like to hear from them why they are seeing me and how I can assist them with their goals. As hard as it may be to believe, everyone does not expect to play well enough to join the PGA Tour. Let's begin your process the same way. I do not believe in people coming to take a series of lessons. My philosophy is to establish a coaching relationship with players. People do not schedule lessons with a teacher; they schedule sessions with their coach. This relationship allows people to establish a process that creates growth in all aspects of the game. I ask you to complete the exercises in this chapter to see where you are before you look to where you are going. This will help you find your personal starting point to begin to *Play REAL Golf.*

Throughout the process it is important to be open and objective. Answer the questions thoroughly and honestly. This may be uncomfortable at times, and that is OK. This will allow you to grow. Have fun with the process and you will have more fun playing golf.

Why Play Golf?

There are a wide variety of reasons that people play golf. Some people want a fun way to be outside and get some exercise. Many people stare at computer screens all day and look to golf as a way to relax.

Some people want a way to spend more time with their families. I love watching parents and children enjoy golf together. Words cannot express the joy that has come from playing golf with my daughters. Golf has allowed us to truly bond. It is phenomenal watching them grow up playing this amazing game.

Many use golf as another way to fuel their competitive drive. Children as young as five years old can play tournament golf. People can then continue to compete long after their football and baseball or basketball careers have ended. As long as air fills your lungs, you can compete.

The business world also brings many people to the game of golf. There is no doubt that many of the biggest business deals are consummated on the golf course. Brian, a player who has grown tremendously by using the *REAL Golf Process*, integrates golf with business in a very interesting way. He first interviews potential sales employees in an office setting and then does his final interview on the golf course. He believes that he can get to know the person much better during a round of golf. Brian also points out that being on the golf course is better than being in an office any day.

Before we can begin establishing goals, we need to do some introspection. We need look at the reasons we play golf and see what commitment we can honestly make to the game.

Knowing your commitment level is the first step to establishing realistic goals for realistic improvement. To expect to perform like a PGA Tour player without ever touching a golf club would be a recipe for frustration and failure. Managing personal expectations that are compatible with your commitment will allow you to build upon your success. This will pave the way for you to grow and improve. *Playing REAL golf* means playing to the best of your personal expectations. Your personal expectations may or may not be based on shooting low scores. There is more to the game of golf than trying to hit 300-yard drives and make 20-foot putts. You need to know what _you_ want to get from playing golf before you can truly bond with the game. To play your best golf you must emotionally connect with the game. Ironically, as the bond develops the drives become longer and more putts drop into the cup.

Exercise #1   Why Play Golf?

A. Why do I (want to) play golf?

_____

_____

_____

_____

_____

_____

B. Realistically, what time and effort can I commit to golf?

_____

_____

_____

_____

_____

_____

_____

_____

_____

_____

C. What positive emotions do you expect to feel when playing golf? Write a statement that describes how good you will feel when playing golf.

_____

_____

_____

_____

_____

_____

_____

Read that phrase every day to reinforce your commitment. Yes, it is ok to read it more than once!

One Game, Different Bodies.

Each of us is gifted with a different body. We all have our physical strengths and weaknesses. Some of us are tall, others are short, some are heavy and some are slight. Some are strong, and others... well, let's just say they aren't bench pressing pick-up trucks. To set a realistic plan for improvement we need to evaluate our physical being and determine if we are satisfied with it. Many people want to get in shape but are unwilling or unable to make lifestyle changes to do so. If you are somebody that has found it difficult or impossible to mold yourself into an athlete or model, this book is perfect for you. Play *REAL* golf can be a catalyst for change, but more importantly, it will optimize your body's performance right now-just as you are!

The *REAL Golf Process* will foster growth regardless of the principles that your lifestyle is based upon or the physical principles that you have used to form your swing.

Exercise #2   One Game, Different Bodies

A. What is the state of my physical being? (What kind of shape am I in?) Do I have any physical limitations?

_____

_____

_____

_____

_____

_____

_____

_____

_____

_____

_____

11

B. Do I have the ability to change any of these limitations? If so, do I realistically plan on doing so? Am I willing to commit to changing my physical limitations? How?

_____

_____

_____

_____

_____

_____

_____

_____

_____

_____

_____

_____

State of the Game Address

You have now had the opportunity to examine why you are playing golf and the state of your physical being. We can now begin to examine your golf game. Many people do not take the time to go through this process. They look for an immediate quick fix, a swing tip or a magical golf club. Within a short period of time, frustration sets in and the attempt to change is abandoned. People want to improve but are unsure of the ways to make effective and lasting changes. The *REAL Golf Process* is the way to get started and create momentum that you can use as a catalyst for success. Building upon your achievement will generate excitement throughout the process. This enthusiasm will motivate you to continue to grow.

As we begin our *REAL Golf Process* it is important to do an evaluation of the current state of your game to establish a workable set of goals and objectives. What are your strengths? What areas are challenges? Can you get the ball in the air?

Exercise #3   <u>Playing *Your* Game</u>

A. What do you enjoy most about golf?

_____

_____

_____

_____

_____

_____

_____

_____

B. What are the best parts of your game?

_____

_____

_____

_____

_____

_____

_____

_____

_____

_____

C. What do you view as your biggest challenge in golf?

_____

_____

_____

_____

_____

_____

_____

_____

D. Are you currently taking lessons or planning to take lessons from a PGA Professional? Why or Why Not?

Many people spend hundreds of dollars on the latest and greatest clubs on the market, yet they do not invest in the knowledge that is necessary to learn how to use the clubs.

_____

_____

_____

_____

_____

_____

_____

_____

_____

You are now ready to "Get REAL!"

We have now examined why you want to play golf and the level of commitment you can make to your game. We have also evaluated your physical being as well as the current state of your game. Now we can begin *the REAL Golf Process* to better golf. *"Let's Get REAL!"*

You can develop your game around whatever goals that you set. Your actions regarding these goals develop your beliefs. Your beliefs then lead to affirming actions that generate productive results. In other words, you act upon what you believe in. Instead of thinking about playing better golf, you will play better golf when you believe that you can.

As a child, our goals and beliefs develop freely regardless of setbacks that befall us. When learning to walk, my daughters would pull themselves up off the ground by reaching up and grabbing anything that was near by: a couch a table, the dog, anything that they could get their hands on. They fell countless times while learning to walk. The dog would walk away and they would fall. They would try to take a few steps away from the couch and they would fall. They continued to try to reach their goal of walking regardless of the setbacks. They did not analyze the movements that it took to be able to walk. They simply got up and tried again because their belief was that they would walk. I am very happy to report that they are walking without issue. Though they do occasionally bump into things.

The beauty of the innocence of childhood is the openness to experience growth. We allow our beliefs to become challenged and we grow more skeptical as we get older. Interestingly, as our attention span gets longer, allowing us to focus on one topic longer, we become more distracted by the setbacks to our beliefs. Often at the first sign of adversity people raise the white flag of surrender. The *REAL Golf Process* will allow you deflect the adversity so you can develop a belief system that fuels itself with productive energy. This positive energy will allow you to navigate the bumps in the road effectively. Much like the child loves the process of learning new things you will grow to enjoy the experience of *the REAL Golf process.*

Has this ever happened to you?

- You are so worried about your end result, you sabotage your round.
- You are so worried about your last shot, you sabotage your round.
- You are so worried about the others in your foursome, you sabotage your round.
- You are so worried about who is watching you, you sabotage your round.

Has this ever happened to you?

- You top your first three shots and give up.
- You convince yourself that you don't deserve to be playing the wonderful course you are playing.
- You convince yourself that you don't deserve to play as well as you are playing.
- You convince yourself that a bad shot during the round means that the rest of your round will be bad.
- You convince yourself that a good shot means that a bad shot is coming next.

You can *REALize* your goals and overcome these common scenarios by committing to the *REAL Golf process*.

The following chapters will demonstrate a step by step process that will help you achieve long lasting improvement in your performance for as long as you play the great game of golf.

Let's examine the way that people process information and how that affects our behavior and performance.

Anatomy of a Behavior
CH. 2

In this Chapter
- ➢ <u>Behavior Elements</u>
- ➢ <u>Positive Words Create Positive Energy</u>
- ➢ <u>Exercises</u>
    - ⇒ **Rephrasing**

Internationally acclaimed personal development authors Doran Andry and "Coach" Joseph McClendon III identify what they call emotional mechanics, the elements that make up the anatomy of peoples' behavior, in their book "The Burning Desire". They have documented the importance of emotions on the behaviors that we exhibit. Our behavior is based upon our emotions.

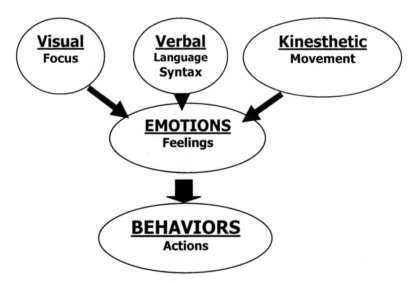

You already know that the way you act is determined by the way you feel. Our emotions are based upon the way we process information. Let's take a look at the "The Anatomy of a Behavior."

The diagram above shows us the way behaviors are formed. Our behaviors (actions) are based upon the emotions (feelings) that are created by the way we process information. We typically have a predominant way of processing information, whether it is visual, verbal, or kinesthetic. Some of us are affected more by what we see, others are affected by what we hear, and yes some are more affected by what we feel. However, all three types of information will have an impact upon our emotions, leading to certain types of behavior. Golf, as we have discussed, is a sports metaphor for life, **so the way that we process information will dictate the <u>emotions that create our performance</u>**.

Let's examine the types of information that we process. The first type we will look at is the information that we process visually. Scientists tell us that our eyes are in the front of our heads for a reason. This goes back to our development as predatory animals. We had to hunt for food, so we had to be able to look outwardly ahead for our prey. After all we had to find food to survive. Studies have shown that we are drawn to and move toward where we are looking. Try to walk a straight line. Good! You can do it. Now, intentionally look to the side as you walk, please walk slowly. You will notice how difficult that it is to do something that you take for granted. The information that we process visually, whether our eyes are open or closed, has a huge impact on us. In other words, what we see or visualize from memory or our imagination creates different emotions that

lead to our behaviors. Take a look at the picture of a sliced lemon.

What happened? Did you pucker up? Did you feel the sour in your mouth and throat? Of course you did, the visualization created the physiological reaction. Photographs can elicit different emotions. I know that if you show me a picture of a juicy steak, I will really taste that steak. Perception is reality.

The way you look at or visualize a golf shot will have an impact on the way you hit the shot. By looking at the shot positively, you create positive emotions that will that allow the positive actions necessary for you to hit the shot well. You hit a good shot based on the way you process the visual input. You must see a good shot before it is hit. Yes, it is that simple.

Verbal information is the second input that we process. Our language, or for our purposes, the words we use, as well as the syntax, the way we use words, will have an impact on the emotions that dictate our behaviors. Simply put, what we say and how we say it will affect the way that we act and the way that others react to us. Scientists have shown us that different words and their use actually create biochemical reactions. However, you don't have to be a scientist to recognize how different words impact us. What do parents say to children when they fall down while trying to learn to walk? Do they call them stupid or clumsy? No, of course not. They praise children for their effort, encouraging them to try again. As adults verbal praise for our efforts remains essential. If you repeatedly hear negative words, you will develop negative emotions that will dictate negative behaviors. Think about the person you know that has a bad day every day. Listen to the way that they talk. They are dominated by negative phrases. On the other hand, if you observe people that seem to be happy all the time, they constantly phrase things positively. The next time you get the opportunity to take a moment to tell someone, "Thank you" or "I appreciate that very much", watch them smile. Your words will have a positive impact on them. An example of how perception of a situation can change is as simple as the way a question is answered. I have taught students that if you do not know the answer to a question, respond by saying, "hmmm" instead of "uhhh". "Hmmm" is perceived as pondering. "Uhhh" is perceived as futility. Again, Perception becomes reality.

Interestingly, we don't even have to say the words out loud for them to affect us. The little voice inside our head or the little person on our shoulder that talks to us has a tremendous impact on how we feel and act. There are times that the little person is helpful and other times that they get us in big trouble. I still have the scar on my leg from the

 little person saying, "Go ahead! You can make it over that fence. Jump!" I wish that was the only time that little voice had given me bad information. There are other times when the "Little Voice" has said pearls of wisdom such as, "You can graduate. Keep studying...just one more hour." If we talk to ourselves positively, we reinforce positive emotions that will lead to positive behaviors. Tell yourself, "Great job!", "Way to go!" or a simple "Yes!" and you will reinforce positive emotions that will lead to improved performance.

The third input is the information that we process kinesthetically. Our movement, posture and body language affect our body's chemicals that change emotions. The way we carry our body and our movement have an affect on the way we feel, and the way we feel will affect our performance.

I can walk in the door and see the way my wife looks at me and know whether I should come and give her a hug, or keep walking out to the dog house. You can sit on a park bench and watch people walk by and tell what emotions they are feeling. It is that obvious! Take a moment and walk over to the nearest mirror. Now, express the meanest scowl you can. Now with the look on your face, try to feel relaxed. Now put the biggest, goofiest grin on your face you can muster. Now, try to feel angry. It is impossible. These simple examples show how important kinesthetic movements are to our emotions.

Our movements have an effect on and are affected by our emotions. Your movements affect your emotions and the emotions of those around you.

A teacher who looks at a class of students made up of some that are leaning back in their chairs and others with their heads on the desk will have to change strategies quickly. The business proposal received by a group that begins to slump or roll their eyes is about to be rejected. Conversely, we have all heard the phrase to sit up and take notice. When something excites us, we change our posture, we are more erect and thus more ready for action. That is why motivational speakers ask their audiences to stand up and move. The positive movements create positive energy. Mom was right, "Stand up straight, you'll feel better". Little did I know, she was helping my golf game.

These examples show how easy it is to observe how others kinesthetically process information. It is not as easy to observe our own body language and physical reactions to information. You must practice positive posture and body language to increase awareness.

Along with our posture, another important factor that affects our body is the amount of oxygen we are processing. When put in stressful situations breathing becomes more shallow and rapid. This decreases the amount of oxygen we process because the lungs are not fully expanding. When my daughters were frightened by something as children, the first step to calming them down was to get them to breathe normally again. They would run to me hyperventilating hysterically. There was no way that they could calm down until they could get oxygen flow. This does not change in adulthood. I vividly remember that after I narrowly avoided a major car accident, that it took at least fifteen minutes to finally get my breathing back to normal. That is why a deep cleansing breath when under stress is so important. The physiological reaction from the additional oxygen helps slow down the body. Take a deep cleansing breath right now and feel how good it feels. Notice that you had to stretch those shoulders back? That is the only way that you can really fill your lungs. Now, smile! After all, you are improving your golf game right now!

All three of these inputs visual, verbal and kinesthetic or what we see, hear and do, affect our emotions, or feelings. Our emotions then dictate our behaviors, or actions, that affect our performance. Most people are aware of the way that they predominantly process information. Unfortunately, the emotions that create behaviors are often ignored. These emotions affect us in the short term as well as  the long term. This is because we are creatures of habit; we tend to behave the same way most of the time. People who ignore emotions, or hide from them, can develop behaviors that have negative short and long term impact on their well-being and health. If we are emotionally down, physically we feel bad. If we are emotionally positive, we feel better physically as well. By increasing awareness of the way we process information, we can create emotions that lead to positive behaviors that improve both our well-being and our performance. Altering the way we process information can create positive emotions that generate fantastic performance. Because of our habitual nature we produce what we reinforce. Reinforcing positive emotions and reducing negative emotions will improve our performance. By creating habits that make us feel good we will produce behaviors that generate better performance that in turn, makes us feel even better. That is why momentum in sports has such a dramatic effect. When you get on a roll, anything is possible! Michael Jordan's Chicago Bulls basketball teams didn't hope to win, they expected to win. Jack Nicklaus finished in the top ten in over 280 of the 594 tournaments he competed in. Byron Nelson won a record 11 PGA Tour events in a row. Why? They created habits that lead to emotions that produced positive results. They then built momentum based upon that success.

Emotional mechanics, those elements that create various behaviors, have a dramatic impact on our golf performance. These emotional mechanics are as vitally important to performance as the physical mechanics of our golf swing. After all, golf is not about having a perfect swing, it is about putting a ball into a hole with the fewest amount of strokes possible.

This was very evident to us while sitting at the par 5, 15th hole at the 2006 Masters Tournament. Many players hit their second shot to the right of the green. It was fascinating to watch the variety of ways that the best players in the world chose to play their third shot. Some played a low running shot, others hit a high soft shot; still others putted the ball. While each chose a different way to play the shot, what they had in common was that they committed to a process that allowed them to play their individual shot to the best of their ability. To improve performance, we must develop positive emotional mechanics.

As we develop our emotional mechanics, it is important to realize that emotions dictate behaviors, in life and in golf.

If you have had a rough day at work and then fight traffic for an hour, I don't care where you arrive as your final destination you will be forced to deal with the stress that you have endured. If seeing your golf coach for a session is your final destination, you will first have to allow yourself to decompress and eliminate the negative energy by replacing it with positive energy. Only then, will you will be able to ever think about your golf game. We eliminate the negative energy by developing positive energy. In other words we have to replace counterproductive emotions with productive emotions. Simple...but not easy to do.

Stress and fear are the greatest causes of negative energy, and this negative energy inhibits our performance. Relaxation and confidence create positive energy, which in turn leads to positive performance. Understanding the importance of processing the information that we see, hear and feel, from a positive perspective is a major step to improving performance. This does not mean that we have to be laughing and giggling. It just means that we have to focus our perspective on the positive information we process.

It is easy to see how processing information negatively affects us on the golf course. If we look at a shot and see a negative target, we fixate on that target. Here is a scenario that many players experience during a round. They look at a hole and see nothing but the water in front of the green (negative visual information). They then hit the shot and there it goes right into the water where they were looking. They then say to themselves, "Nice shot dummy!" (negative verbal information) and then their shoulders collapse and they slump down as they throw down another ball in disgust (negative kinesthetic information). While still calling themselves a variety of names they hit the next shot...Any wonder why that ball also splashes into the water? The negative visual, verbal and kinesthetic movements all led to negative emotions which inhibited performance. By continuing the pattern, performance cannot improve.

We eliminate these negative visual, verbal and kinesthetic movements when *playing REAL Golf*. A *REAL player* focuses their eyes **only** on where they want the ball to go. They do not try to ignore the water on a hole, they know that it is there. They **choose to focus** on the target and by focusing on their target, the water fades out of existence. The water will not affect them negatively because they are positively committed to the target. They then say to themselves, "I like this club, it is perfect for this yardage." Before taking a practice swing, they take a deep cleansing breath and stand with good posture. They then take a good practice swing and then launch the ball right on the green. Of course, the big smile after the shot and saying "Yes!" reinforces the good shot. The good shot is a result of positively processing the visual, verbal and kinesthetic movements. The positive emotions created by processing the information positively produced positive performance. As a result, you build momentum for your next shot!

The *REAL Golf Process* will allow you to commit to improving your performance based upon your success instead of error correction. It's simple, not easy. All you have to do is keep it REAL.

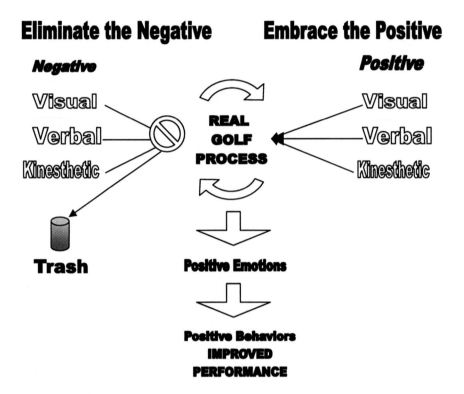

You can deflect negative information and integrate positive information with the *REAL Golf Process*.

This allows you to focus on positive emotions that improve performance.

Positive Words Create Positive Energy

The words we use are very powerful. Scientists are now documenting the power of neurolinguistics in sports. The manner of our expression and the style of phrasing we use can be called syntax. In other words, it's not just the words we use but how we choose to use them that determines their impact. If we use negative syntax we create negative images that of course create negative energy. Using positive syntax creates positive energy; this positive energy allows us to perform optimally.

We have all come across people in our lives who can find the negative in any situation. I knew a person who once won an all expense paid trip to Hawaii. Instead of being excited, all he talked about was that he was going to have to pay additional income tax because of the trip. Needless to say, his trip was not enjoyable. The words that he used throughout the trip created nothing but negative energy. I am still waiting to win a trip like that; you can bet I would enjoy it!

How many times have you stopped and said to someone "Hi, how are you?" and had the person automatically reply "Oh, I am fine, how are you?" The auto-response is almost void of positive energy. This void leaves the person wide open for an attack of negativity. Dealing with this negative energy drains them of any positive energy they may have. It sucks the life out of them. I refuse to allow negativity to get into my system. I protect myself against the negativity around me by using only positive syntax. I sometimes shock people with my positive response, "Any better and it would be illegal!" Try it some time; it is worth seeing the reaction from the checker at the grocery store. They will inevitably smile. The amazing thing is that this energy is contagious, the more positive that I am, the more positive those around me become.

This principle works during your round of golf also. Phrasing all statements, ESPECIALLY what you say to YOURSELF, as positive statements creates positive energy to build on. As mentors of mine say "Repetition is the mother of skill, but Reward is the father of success." Reward yourself after good shots with positive comments. This can be as simple as "Yes!" or "Golf shot!" or "Great stroke!" These statements while simple, are so powerful that they can create success that fosters even more success. "Phenomenal!" is the word that Megan and Amanda use after a good shot. These college players have found that the more that they say, "Phenomenal" the more good shots they hit!

Negative syntax allows the negative energy to creep in and bring you down. For example, an accomplished player that has embraced the *REAL Golf Process* used to say "Nice shot dummy, you call yourself a golf pro!" after hitting a shot below his expectations. This comment served to reaffirm that he could not play well. The scary part was that he did it so often; he didn't even recognize that he was saying it. Through the *REAL Golf Process* he has developed an entire repertoire of statements that serve as an exclamation to relieve the stress. However, they reinforce that he is a good player who simply hit a shot below his expectations. He has replaced the negative phrase with comments like "Wow, who hit that shot?" or "That is not like me at all!" By replacing the negative phrases he has been able to let go of the bad shot and prepare for the upcoming shot. As a result, he hits fewer shots that would bring the negative phrases and is instead praising himself for good shots.

I'll be honest with you that at first this will seem very artificial. During sessions, I'll step out in front of players after a shot to wait for a person to reward themselves. They will look at me perplexed and then you can see the smile come on their face, as they say "Oh yeah, I remember...YES! They seem embarrassed at first to reward themselves with a hearty "Yes!" But much like a grip change, the more you practice using it, the more natural it becomes. The good news is you will be hitting fewer shots below your expectations and instead of these negative comments you will be saying "Yes" to more good shots.

Rephrasing exercise

This exercise will help you develop ways to practice rephrasing the commentary you say about your shots during a round. To perform this exercise you may need some help from your friends. You may be unaware of the comments that you make, but your friends will remember. Record between 5 to 10 negative comments you made during your last round of golf. If you made more than 10, deal with the additional comments by repeating the exercise.

Part 1.

      A. Record each negative comment and the hole or shot that you faced at that moment.

_____

_____

_____

_____

_____

_____

_____

_____

_____

_____

_____

B. Write down a different comment that could be phrased positively to replace the negative.

_____

_____

_____

_____

_____

_____

_____

_____

_____

_____

C. Practice saying the positive comment!

Yes it is artificial at first. Repetition is the key.

It gets easier every time you do it.!

Part 2.

A. Record each positive comment and the hole or shot you faced at that moment.

_____

_____

_____

_____

_____

_____

_____

_____

_____

_____

B. Practice saying the positive comments.

Yes, repetition is the key.

It gets easier every time you do it!

The REAL Golf Process
CH. 3

In this Chapter

You now should have a much better understanding of why it is imperative to process visually, verbally and kinesthetically to create positive emotions. These positive emotions will then generate positive behaviors that improve performance. Seeing, hearing, and feeling information through a positive process will make you feel good. These good feelings will help you play better. People that attend a professional tournament are often surprised to see that the pros attempt to do the same thing before each shot. The most successful players are those who are able to execute a *positive process* during their round. The *REAL Golf Process* will provide you a system that you can use on a daily basis to ensure that you are creating the positive emotions necessary to perform at your best. The process has four steps; Relax, Evaluate, Activate and Let it Go.

R- Relax

Much like many areas of life golf offers many interesting paradoxes. According to statistics the #1 reason people play golf is to relax. Yet the #1 problem people have while playing is difficulty in relaxing. Golf is one of the few sports that players must balance effort with relaxation. For many people the harder you try the worse the results. Yet if you relax and just swing away, everything falls into place. I would love to have a dollar for every time I have heard "the harder I try the harder it gets." Stephen has a great phrase that he uses in sessions, "double the pause...half the effort." Reducing tension allows the body to operate efficiently. In other words the more we can relax and allow our body to, "do what it knows how to do", the better you will play. It has been said many times, "You don't play golf to relax, you relax to play golf."

Basketball players can win by playing harder on defense. Football players can win by hitting someone harder. The more effort that the players put in, the better their performance becomes. Golf however requires a balance between effort and relaxation. I have had many players describe their rounds as tight at the beginning of the round, sloppy in the middle of the round, then they say "as soon as I said to myself just to forget about everything and just play, I did really well." The golf paradox is that if we work too hard to create the proper golf swing, or we try too hard to make a chip or putt, we create unnecessary tension that is self-defeating. Tension, whether it comes from nervousness or simply trying too hard is damaging to the mechanics of the golf swing. Tension, believe it or not, also makes us weaker. Friend and mentor Dr. Jon Gundlach, the man who keeps both Stephen and I moving as well as possible, always says, "A tight muscle is a weak muscle." This is where the game is simple but not easy. We must find the balance of effort and relaxation. It is conceptually simple to relax and swing to put the white ball into a hole, but it certainly is not easy.

Many people take lessons to improve and they have a professional put them through a series of uncomfortable movements and then say, "that's it relax". "Sure"....they say... "Yeah right". Golfers often find themselves in uncomfortable circumstances, competing in tournaments, playing with the boss or clients, people they don't know or sometimes the most uncomfortable friends and family. Play golf in those circumstances and relax... yeah right.

Actually the answer is yeah right! Relax and enjoy. Simple answer but not easy.

Relaxation comes from understanding the circumstances that you are in and creating positive energy around them. Recently Jeff, a successful athlete who has recently begun to play golf, came up and gave me a big high five and said, "You're going to be proud of the way I am hitting, I'm finally relaxing and letting it go!"

During my high school basketball coaching career, I was fortunate to coach with incredibly talented coaches and players. During that ten year period we won several championships. I still proudly wear the first California State Title Ring. These talented high school players had the privilege of playing the championship games in NBA and College arenas. As coaches, we took an interesting way to relax the players. Usually coaches want the players to have tunnel vision, focusing only on the playing of the game. This can lead to playing tight in big games. The tension from the focus defeats the ability to perform.

Instead of allowing the players to create the tension from the intimidation of the arena we took them to a place that relieved the tension and made it comfortable. We took them to the arenas before the game and showed them the enormity of the building. We shared with them the excitement of the opportunity of the game and that the energy from the building would be distributed differently than the gyms that we had always played in. Each player visualized what they would feel walking out onto the floor. During the warm ups they were told to make sure and look around the arena and soak in the energy. The players were able to experience the wider views of the court, the sounds and yes, the energy. We took the possibility of negativity and eliminated it before it could even get started. We took tension and created positive energy.

When playing golf it is important to eliminate the negative energy of tension before it can grow into a monster by creating positive energy. During one of their epic British Open showdowns, Tom Watson turned to Jack Nicklaus and said, "Is this great or what?" Tom recognized the tension of the situation and chose to enjoy the moment.

When David, a former member of my California Interscholastic Federation (CIF) Championship golf team was preparing to play in the U.S. Open qualifier for the first time we spent a lot of time preparing for the nerves that could show up in an important tournament. He visualized and talked about good shots that he had hit in previous tournaments. He also practiced looking around the golf course and recognizing the beauty of the course. The result was one to build upon, he qualified for the sectionals.

You can enjoy the moment by recognizing what causes the tension and replacing it with positive thoughts and energy. The more you practice taking stressful situations and turning them into positive situations, the easier that it will become. This practice is beneficial on the golf course and will also pay dividends in the business world, and will help improve personal relationships.

Tension Recognition Exercise

The following exercise is to allow you to recognize what is causing tension or anxiety during various situations. By recognizing the cause of the negative emotions you can then logically prove to yourself why those emotions are invalid and should be replaced with valid constructive emotions.

The two examples below show how you can take anxious situations and turn them into relaxed confident ones using REAL principles. The REAL grid takes you through a rational process that describes:

- The anxious situation

- Your negative feelings about the situation

- The negative thoughts that accompany that feeling

- The evidence that supports the negative thoughts and feelings

- Actions that you have taken that disprove the negative thoughts and feelings

- Positive thoughts that you develop based upon the actions you have taken

- Relaxed Confidence that has now replaced the negative.

The first example focuses on the nerve racking situation of playing golf with the boss.

Example (golf course)

Situation	Playing with the Boss
Feelings	Nervous
Negative Thoughts	Don't embarrass yourself!
Supporting Evidence	Bad shots of last round
Disproving Actions	Success using the *REAL GOLF PROCESS*
Alternative Positive Thoughts	Have Fun! Boss will see me in a new light.
REAL Feelings	Relaxed Confidence

The second example focuses on a common problem faced by many people in their every day life. Test Anxiety!

Example (daily life)

Situation	Final Exam
Feelings	Nervous
Negative Thoughts	I'm a poor test taker
Supporting Evidence	Failed test in past
Disproving Actions	New study habits, tutoring, positive focus from practicing the *REAL Golf Process*
Alternative Positive Thoughts	*REAL Golf Process* with good study habits will lead to *REAL* Results
REAL Feelings	REAL Confidence

Now you practice. Complete the exercise using two situations that you face; one in your daily life and one in golf. Make sure that you write your answers. Taking the time to write this down completes this as a valid exercise. This will help you begin the *REAL Golf Process* and you will be able to confidently RELAX.

Situation	
Feelings	
Negative Thoughts	
Supporting Evidence	
Disproving Actions	
Alternative Positive Thoughts	
<u>*REAL*</u> *Feelings*	

Situation	
Feelings	
Negative Thoughts	
Supporting Evidence	
Disproving Actions	
Alternative Positive Thoughts	
<u>REAL</u> Feelings	

How to further relax during a round of golf will be discussed later in the chapter The REAL Golf Shot Process. One of the best ways to promote relaxation is a simple one, remember to breathe.

E- Evaluate

When most people think of evaluating the circumstances of a golf shot they think of the yardage, the lie, wind, the surrounding hazards waiting to steal the ball. All of these things are very important, but the perspective in which you are doing the evaluation will affect what you see.

When people view life, the perspective in which they look determines their evaluation of the situation. Some people look at a painting by Picasso and marvel at its artistic splendor, others like me look at it and ask, "What is that?" In other words, how you look at the yardage, how you look at the lie, how you view the shot itself will affect your evaluation of that playing situation. When playing REAL golf you will evaluate the circumstances that you face with each shot through a vision of positive energy. Through practice you can evaluate each shot and putt positively. It will take practice, but just as I have learned a better appreciation of art, you can see positives in each shot you play. This process begins for each shot as soon as the club has been put away from the preceding shot. As you approach the ball evaluate the surroundings of the shot you next face. By minimizing your tunnel vision you will enhance your enjoyment of the game because you will be able to enjoy the beauty and grace of the golf course and the nature of the course.

Playing in the 2005 Nissan Open Pro-Am, while walking to my ball on the 496 yard Par 4 15th hole, one of the most difficult holes on the course I found myself looking at the enormous Eucalyptus trees to check the wind. I turned to my dear friend and caddy Jerry and said, "Can you believe how beautiful this is? He replied, "It doesn't get much better than this." Not only is Riviera Country Club one of the most famous and historic golf courses in the world, it is visually gorgeous. Riviera is one of the most popular stops on the PGA Tour. Some might say that I had lost focus; I maintain that I allowed myself to enjoy the golf which reduced tension and allowed me to perform. I hit the second shot where I wanted to and made a solid par. We evaluated a negative situation through a positive vision.

While playing in the tournament the year before, throughout the round, every time I hit a shot Jerry being a great caddie said, "We hit a good one there, great chance for us to make birdie here." That was until the 12th hole when I pulled a drive into the left trees. As we approached the ball, in my evaluation process I turned to him and said, "What are we going to do here? He replied with a laugh, "We...We...You hit it here!" We both laughed, played the safe shot, laying up to about 110 yards from there got up and down for par.

Both of these situations could have led to increased tension and led to disaster. By evaluating the shots positively I allowed myself to perform with reduced tension which gave me success to build upon.

Evaluation exercise

Everyone looks at situations in different ways. Stephen is a passionate fisherman. On the many different golf courses that he plays Stephen looks at lakes and wonders about all the fishing opportunities. Others look at the lakes and see all the ways that their golf ball could end up at the bottom. How you look at the situation affects the way you deal with them. One of the greatest vacations of his life was a trip to Montana with his lovely wife Holly. The memories of that trip remain fresh in his mind today. When he sees the lake he reinforces the good memories of fly fishing on the Madison River. The calmness that he feels allows him to relax and deal with the shot at hand, without the anxiety of missing the shot into the water. He has evaluated it in a way that allows him to relax.

For those of you who don't fish, and there are a few of us. You can still look at the situation without anxiety. Look at the wildlife, the beauty of the landscape. Realize the beauty of the natural surroundings of the golf course, and then allow yourself to evaluate the shot at hand. You are done evaluating the lake. Move on, evaluate where you want the ball to go. In other words you have recognized the presence of the water and then you move beyond it.

Through practice you can evaluate situations in a different manner. This will mean changing your perspective, not what you are looking at. This will be unnatural at first, because it is different. It is ok to feel some discomfort when beginning this process.

Recognizing the difference of perspective will allow the growth. Your perspective will allow you to evaluate things positively. You will become more comfortable with the change in perspective the more you practice.

Evaluate the previous picture above in two perspectives.

- Write down the negatives that you see in one column and the positives in the other.

Negatives	Positives

- Now choose which of the positives you can narrow down to your main focus.

- That becomes the basis of your perspective.

- Now look at the picture again from the positive perspective you have established.

- Practice evaluating all of the situations you face through a positive perspective.

The Eyes have it

Evaluating each situation through a positive perspective can only happen through an effective visualization process. Visualization is a very powerful tool. There is no doubt that we go where we are looking. Personal Development experts have used visualization tools to help people reach their goals

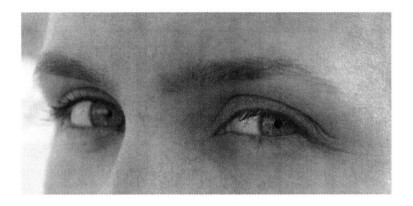

using tools such as dream charts, affirmation notes, or a multitude of others designed to have people look at where they want to go. Seeing yourself accomplishing goals when they are established is the first step to success. Through out the years of coaching high school golf there was one team that exemplified the visualization process.

The 2002 Woodbridge High School boy's golf team used visualization to successfully separate themselves from others. It was a very talented group of young men that worked together toward a goal of a championship. They competed against incredibly talented teams in Southern California. They were smart enough to know that their individual performance would not be enough to win a team championship. Collectively they knew that they would need more than just individual talent to reach their team goals. We decided that we would focus on positive imagery, both long term and short term. Before and after practice rounds we practiced tricky chips and pitches to visualize these shots being hit in competition. We visualized together warming up on the practice range of the course we were going to play before our first day of practice. We were going to be the first team on the range, wearing our all black uniforms...to intimidate according to the players. We would warm up on the far right hand side of the range so we would only deal with our process and all of the other teams would have to watch us prepare. We then visualized holding the plaque that the winning team would receive. We went so far as to visualize the meal we would eat to celebrate after the tournament.

We visualized this before practice sessions and during team meetings. The feelings we would experience, the sights, the smells, the sounds of success. We then discussed what visualization would be necessary on a day to day shot by shot basis to reach those goals.

Still today the young men talk about that winning season. The bond that they share of reaching the common goal is one that will endure the ages as will the rings that they wear to symbolize the championship. More importantly, they continue to talk about the power of the visualization and that as men they visualize success as they reach for their life goals.

Players and coaches of championship teams in all sports use visualization to reach goals. Greatness can only come by seeing it first! After all we can only go where we see. Mentors say that this is the true reason that our eyes are on the front of our head. Choose to see success and you will reach your goals. It is just that simple. Simple yes... but not easy. Skeptics say that they look for the worst to happen, so they are never disappointed. Those people are reaching for the heights of mediocrity. You will see the positive results before they happen. Play REAL Golf will teach you how to practice visualization. Practicing the visualization process will help you build upon your success. You will develop the ability to see your positive visualization when you need it most, during stressful situations. The following exercise teaches you how to visualize positively and set triggers to release those positive emotions upon demand.

Visualization Exercise

I have heard countless times from players that they missed a shot because they never felt good about the shot. They were unsure about what club, the lie, the shape of the shot or any of a multitude of things. I have also heard players comment that they knew they were going to miss a putt before they have hit it. "I knew that I was going to miss that"... "I could have told you that was coming".

As part of the evaluation portion of our process you will

use visualization to create good shots based upon a "treasure chest of good shots" stored in your memory. Each good shot that you hit will be saved in your memory to build success for future shots. These memories of good shots, or "treasure chest of shots" are used to build confidence in the shot that you are going to hit during a round. To hit a good shot you must commit to the visualization that you create. You will be able to commit to the shot that you want to hit because of the positive energy created through this visualization. You will feel confident because you have hit that shot well before.

After you hit a good shot set a trigger to release that emotion upon demand. This trigger can be as simple as closing your fist and saying yes! Your trigger can be anything that you are comfortable with. It is important to make it a physical movement (kinesthetic) as well as a verbal cue (syntax). By using both physical and verbal cues the trigger will be strengthened.

A. Describe one of the best shots you have ever hit.

_____

_____

_____

_____

_____

_____

_____

_____

_____

B. Close your eyes and feel what you experienced.
Write down what you felt.

_____

_____

_____

_____

_____

_____

_____

C. Write some words that describe the emotions that you
feel.

_____

_____

_____

_____

_____

D. Write down a trigger that you can use to recall that positive visualization. ***The trigger can be anything that you are comfortable using consistently!***

_____

_____

_____

_____

_____

_____

_____

_____

_____

Activate

Preparing ourselves to complete tasks is an important step to ensure success. Actors and speakers rehearse their performances. Astronauts go through countless hours of checklist practice. Coaches play out every scenario that they can imagine to prepare game plans.

A round of golf is typically played in four to five hours. The action of hitting a golf shot actually only takes about three seconds. That means that during the four to five hours

on the golf course, the actual amount of time executing shots for the average player is about six minutes. <u>Yes, only six minutes</u>. That means that we are spending much more time preparing for shots than playing them.

When playing REAL golf you will treat each shot that you hit as a separate event. After all, very few people can focus on anything for five hours. Rehearsing the movements that you want to create will ensure that your mind and body are ready to perform. Often this comes down to playing ten seconds at a time. When players tell me that they lose focus during a round, they are often surprised when I let them know that it is all right. It is important to know that all you have to do is to <u>activate your body for ten seconds at a time</u>. Again repetition is the mother of skill. Repeating the same activation process will allow you to be optimally prepared to perform your best. Golf is a game to be enjoyed, allow yourself the pleasure of being on the golf course. Activate your body to perform when you need to.

Let it Go!

Once prepared to play a shot or hit a shot all that is left to do is let it go. Allow your body to perform with positive energy, absent of tension and negative energy. The reason athletes practice is to allow them to perform at game time. By activating your golf swing with a purposeful practice swing you can clear your mind and go into auto-pilot.

Sure, you say, remember all of the movements necessary to hit a shot and then relax. See this, do this, do that, focus on this, adjust this and oh yeah, relax while you do it. You know you have a complex kinesthetic motion to make that you need to focus on each part. Relax? Well, yes. You are not just going to hit a golf shot you will hit a REAL shot!

Allowing your body to perform refers to repeating what you have done in the activate mode. If you try to make corrections in the swing during the swing, it will lead to an aborted mission. It is very important to remember that if you are unsure or uncomfortable, start the process again. If you change the shot decision you have made, give your body time to commit to the decision. There are no balks in golf. By repeating the activate mode you will be able to efficiently use the positive energy that you have created to hit a REAL shot.

Once the shot is hit or the putt has been stroked it is over, you must let it go once the club returns to your bag.

In other words you must accept the results of the shot and move on to the next shot. Again, simple...but not easy. Repetition will be the key. The more that you can allow your body to perform without tension the better your performance will be.

Many people spend more time thinking about the shot they hit two holes before or the shot coming up three holes ahead. This does nothing to help your performance, it distracts and creates tension. You will have plenty of chances to talk about the shots that you hit after your round.

I've heard stories about a golf legend in Texas. When he was asked what he thought about during his backswing. He replied, "You don't think about eating a steak, you just eat it." "I just do it."

Let's revisit my daughters learning to walk. Walking is a very complicated physiological movement. All children fall down repeatedly when first walking. When they hit the ground they may cry for a short period of time, but before you know it they are back up trying again. My daughters didn't worry about what they had done wrong when they fell. They didn't study the last attempt and try to figure out what they had done wrong. They got up and tried to get to their next destination, fell, got up, fell until they mastered the balance required to walk. Ask yourself, did you study books or videos on how to walk? Did you try to analyze the movement of walking? No, you simply got up, and went to where you were trying to go. As children we are able to let go of set backs quickly, the failure of walking is forgotten almost immediately, the focus becomes the next goal.

Golf is a game. It should be viewed in a child like manner. Let go and allow the body to do what it is supposed

to do. If you face a set back, get over it quickly and move the focus to the next goal. All you really have to do is find the ball and figure out a way to try to get it in the hole with the next shot.

The REAL Shot Process
CH. 4

In this Chapter

- ➤ **The REAL Shot Process**
- ➤ **Ten Seconds at a Time**
- ➤ **Remaining in the REAL Golf Process**
- ➤ **Evaluating Your Round**
- ➤ **Exercises**
    - ⇒ **Breathing**
    - ⇒ **Practice Tee**
    - ⇒ **REAL Scorecard**

Ten Seconds at a Time

Many of you are saying, "OK, this all seems to make sense. Positive energy creates positive results. Negative energy inhibits performance. Great! How do I use this information and make it work for me?" Through the many years that I have spent with players I have seen a lot of different types of swings and a lot of different ways to putt. I have seen talented players implode and marginally talented players win by scoring better than anybody expected. The difference between success and disappointment has been the players' ability to work their process.

A former team captain Jake always loved playing in the last group in team matches. He said that he loved the idea of being in the anchor group because, "if it is close, there is no way they can beat my process." He was right; his positive outlook to every shot made him a tough opponent in team play. He didn't lose a high school match over a two year period. The main reason that Jake began to play in this position was the mentoring that  Stephen provided. He had played in the same anchor position for his college team because his coach could count on Stephen's process. They won two Conference Championships and one State Title with Stephen anchoring the team.

We have created a simple process that you can use for **every shot of every round of golf**. This process will allow you to perform at your best on and off the golf course by incorporating positive visual, verbal and kinesthetic input. In other words focusing on positive things with our eyes, ears, and the rest of our body we will build performance that will guarantee success. This is where you get to apply what you have learned. You can *KEEP IT REAL!*

R- Relax

It is very evident that when people are afraid or nervous. They are nearly hyperventilating, and at times, actually hyperventilating. They speak quickly and their hands tremble.

When people are angry, it is just as easy to see. The body either tenses or completely slumps. Both nervousness and anger are emotions that are based upon negative energy. On the other hand confidence is also easy to see. You can see the person walk and talk with purpose. Confidence is based upon relaxation. Relaxation comes from the positive energy of being positively focused. REAL players are confident because they have a process that is proven to ensure reliable performance. Yet regardless of the confidence that you have, everyone can become tense. Yes, every time that I tee it up for a tournament or a corporate outing, after decades of playing golf I have to remind myself to relax. The easiest way to enhance relaxation is to breathe.

As simple as it seems, people forget to breathe. The next time you see someone who is upset, observe how shallow their breathing is. By denying the body oxygen the ability to perform at our optimum level is inhibited.

Before each shot, starting with the first tee shot, take a nice slow deep breath and allow the oxygen to cleanse your system. Yes, it is that simple. Put your shoulders back and take a deep breath. Adding oxygen to your system will immediately allow your brain to function more efficiently. This will also allow you to flush any negative energy out of the system. If you need a couple of deep breaths, it is O.K. to take more than one.

As we have established we are creatures of habit. If you create a habit of taking a deep breath to begin the shot process, you are giving your body the cue that it is game time. The ten seconds that you are going to perform is beginning.

Exercise #1 Breathing Exercise

Stand up, go ahead no one is looking. Put your shoulders back and take a deep breath. Feel the cleansing of your system. Go on do it once more. It feels good doesn't it?

E- Evaluate

Evaluate what you are facing at this moment. Nothing else matters, not earlier shots on holes, nor those to follow. What do I need to do right here, right now? The car wash can wait, the email is going to be there after the shot.

This stage of the process actually begins as you approach your ball. In this stage you evaluate the shot at hand. Where are you going to hit the shot? How far do you need to go? Wind, lie, atmospheric conditions are all accounted for and a decision is made of the type of shot that you are going to play. There will be some situations that you will take aim directly at the flag, other situations will dictate that you aim at other places, such as the safe side of the green.

In this part of the process you need to evaluate the shot in your own terms. What is your margin of error? PGA Tour professionals have the ability to hit shots very close to

where they are aiming. Recreational players need to give themselves more room for error. If a pin is tucked in a corner of a green near a hazard, a tour professional may aim just right of the pin. Recreational players should be aimed at the right side of the green, after all a shot anywhere on the green would be considered a good shot. It is important to put aside your ego and be realistic. This will allow you to positively focus on your target, instead of allowing the negative energy to creep in.

When evaluating putts, it is important to concentrate on the <u>distance</u> you want the ball to travel first. What speed do you need the ball to travel? Then see the path of the ball going into the hole. Looking at edges will lead to hitting edges.

Once you have evaluated the conditions you **must** **commit** to the type of shot that you are going to play. You can only perform if you have committed to the action. Like anything else in life you have to commit to your objectives before you can reach them. My grandfather had a great way

to describe commitment. He used to talk about people who were always going to do something, but they never committed to success. They never found success because they did not commit. He used to tell me to take a look at breakfast, specifically bacon and eggs....The Chicken was involved, the Pig committed. He was right, you must commit to success before you can succeed.

Once you have committed to your shot reinforce it by verbally confirming your commitment.

If you are playing with a caddie, tell the caddie the shot you plan to hit.

Of course you don't have to have a caddie to do this. You can tell yourself the same thing. The evaluation and commitment to the type of shot you will play will take place before you have touched your bag or clubs. It is very important that you commit to the shot you will play. Recently, Stephen volunteered to caddie for one of his up and coming junior players.

Prior to every shot his mantra was "commit, before you hit". The player was sixteen shots better over the two days than she was the previous year at the same tournament. That is *keeping it REAL*, thanks to a great caddie!

A- Activate

You have visualized the shot or putt, where the ball will go and how it will get there. You have verbally confirmed your commitment to the shot. Now it is time to prepare your body for the shot or putt you are about to make.

It is vital to make consistent rehearsal swings for every shot that you hit. Often players forget this important step after hitting a shot that was below their standards. I have worked with players that take great practice swings on the practice tee and then never take a purposeful practice swing after they have hit the first shot on the course.

Take a practice stroke or swing to prepare you for that particular shot. Your practice swing is a rehearsal of the successful shot you are about to hit. The type of shot you will be hitting will dictate the type of practice swing you will take.

For example, if you are trying to hit a low shot into the wind the practice swing should rehearse that shot with a low finish, with the appropriate club. Is it logical to take your driver out and swing it just before you hit a shot from a bunker? No. Activating the practice swing that you need for the ten seconds of performance gives the body the kinesthetic input it needs to make a good shot.

Exercise #2 Activation Process Exercise

Each player consciously or through their sub-conscious goes through a process prior to hitting a shot or making a putt. REAL golfers will use the exact same process for every shot that they hit. This will allow the mind and body to perform. The process should be something that you feel comfortable with doing each shot that you hit. Later I will describe the components of the shot process that includes the REAL elements. The process will be a work in progress and it will vary based upon your individuality. The key is that the process should remain the same throughout the round of golf. What the process is does not matter, the key is to do the same procedure that will allow you to "commit and hit".

A. Describe the current process that you use before each shot. If you cannot describe it go to B.

_____

_____

_____

_____

_____

_____

_____

_____

B. Create a process that you will feel comfortable with for each shot that you hit and write it.

_____

_____

_____

_____

_____

_____

_____

_____

_____

_____

C. Practice the process with every shot you hit through 15 minute practice sessions. Yes, only 15 minute sessions.

A1. Describe the current process that you use before each putt. If you cannot describe it go to B1.

_____

_____

_____

_____

_____

_____

_____

_____

B1. Create a process that you will feel comfortable with for each putt that you stroke. Write down what you will do for each putt.

_____

_____

_____

_____

_____

_____

_____

_____

_____

_____

_____

_____

_____

C3. Practice the process with every putt you hit through 15 minute practice sessions. How do you feel?

_____

_____

_____

_____

L- *Let it Go!*

You have visually and verbally prepared your body for what you want to do. You have activated the body with a rehearsal of what to do. Now comes the easy part. Clear your mind and allow your body to perform. You can clear your mind and swing because your preparation is complete. Simply put, *"Let it go!"* That's right, quit thinking, your mind and body are prepared, all you have to do is *"Let it go!"*

Several REAL players have used the metaphor of sending a computer document to the printer. You have typed it up, and all you have to do is hit "print", the computer takes it from there.

Once the shot is played, it is over. Those ten seconds of performance have ended. You cannot rewind the tape for another result. Unless you are playing with your boss, they get unlimited mulligans of course! We however, must accept the results and move forward.

It is important to reward yourself for a good shot. This can be as simple as closing your fist and saying "yes". As we have said, we are creatures of habit. Positive reinforcement will lead to future positive results. Golf is not a game that you will hit every shot to your expectations. Everyone will make mechanical errors occasionally, as much as it may shock you even the authors of this book do not hit every shot exactly how we want to. Tour players do not hit every shot perfectly. There will also be times that you mechanically play a shot the way you want to but have made a misjudgment in planning. We have to accept the results and move forward. Simple...but not easy.

By having a process to rely on we can let a poor shot go. If the shot is below your performance standards make a positive comment or a silly comment such as "who hit that?" then take a swing, feeling what you wanted to do and put the club away. The key is that the ten seconds of performance ends when the club goes back into your bag. When the club is back in your bag it means that shot is over, whether it was up to your standards or not. Let it go and begin the process for

the next shot. This will prevent one bad shot from leading to another or as many people experience one bad hole killing a round. Evaluation of the round will be dealt with after the round is complete. Believe it or not, you need to practice putting your club in your bag to end the process.

If you made a swing that is short of expectations being aware of thoughts that interfered with the swing allows you to change them. Schmitty, a committed student of the *Play REAL Golf Process* had to learn how to eliminate analysis paralysis. This is a guaranteed recipe for a poor round of golf. This usually comes from making swing changes on each swing. Trying to correct the swing each time creates negative energy that detracts from your performance. The time for a lesson is before your next round, not during this round. It is important to create selective amnesia; shots you didn't hit well are eliminated from your memory. It is much like deleting a computer file. There is no need to take up valuable memory space that can be used to remember good shots.

The PGA Teaching Manual describes seven principles for good putting; however it describes only 3 things necessary for a successful putt. Putter is square to the putting line; putt is on the right path, at the right speed.

If you tried to thinks about 7 things and have a soft touch it would be paralyzing. Following the *REAL Golf Process* frees you from the mechanical issues and allows you to focus on right distance and the right path. This freedom will allow you to be confident in the putts that you stroke. Remembering the importance of syntax (our words), if you stroked the putt on the path you wanted to with the speed that you wanted to, you have made the putt, regardless of whether the ball drops into the hole or not. Focusing on your process will reduce the interference and allow you to perform your best. The *REAL Golf Process* is a recipe for success.

I recently played at a fantastic private corporate outing at the world renowned Olympic Club in San Francisco, with John (known as Johnny Hands) a committed student of the *REAL Golf Process*. While flying back, as we were talking about the amazing day, John had a very poignant comment. He said that while playing golf with me that he was always surprised at how much I talked to myself out loud. When we first started working together it sounded like I was making excuses during the round. "Good stroke, I hit that right where I wanted, almost went in." "Good swing, guess the wind gusted." These were two examples of comments from that day's round. John now understood why I talked to myself so much. He understood that I was rewarding myself for good performance, even if the result was not exactly what I wanted. By rewarding myself for what I had done well I was able to build upon the positive energy. He went on to say that his performance had really improved since rewarding himself for good process.

This process is deep in its explanation yet simple in action; it can be done very quickly on the course. You can relax and evaluate the shot as you approach the ball. Committing to the shot can be done immediately upon completing the evaluation. A purposeful practice swing, which prepares the body for action will lead to the shot. You have created an efficient system to play your game. Your process is individualized for you.

Exercise #3 Practice Tee Exercise

It now time to begin implementing the *REAL Golf Process* with every shot you play. To begin, take the book with you to your next practice session. Open the book to the following page. Play three shots using the process.

Write down the positive feelings you had when playing the shots. It is important to remember that the result of the shot itself is not what matters, it is the positive feelings you had while playing the shots that will reinforce your process.

R- *Relax*
Take a deep breath with your shoulders back.

E- *Evaluate*
Choose a target, check the wind conditions and commit to the type of shot that you are going to play

A- *Activate*
Take a practice swing that is a rehearsal swing for the shot

L- *Let it Go!*
Clear your mind and allow the swing to happen.

Shot #1 Positive Feelings

_____

_____

_____

_____

_____

_____

Shot#2   Positive Feelings

_____

_____

_____

_____

_____

_____

Shot#3   Positive Feelings

_____

_____

_____

_____

_____

_____

It is OK to feel uncomfortable when first completing this exercise. You should repeat this exercise for at least three shots of every practice session until you are completely comfortable with the process. Build upon these positive feelings. Every shot of every practice session and every shot of every round will be played with this process. If you find yourself out of your process simply start again on the next shot that you are going to play. Performance will improve because of the positive emotions created and the process will become a good habit. The result will be better shots during each practice session and more importantly better shots in every round that you play.

Remaining in the *REAL* Golf Process

On a recent corporate outing at the fantastic Bandon Dunes Golf Resort, I watched a player hit a lob wedge 180 yards...the only problem was that he only wanted the ball to travel 50 yards. It was actually pretty funny, we still laugh about it. While walking up to the green, from the middle of the fairway (for the second time), he said, "All I could think about over the ball was, I can't hit this shot. Boy was I right." He then returned to his process and saved his double bogey with a good putt.

How can players remain in the process when negative thoughts attempt to overtake them? Many people are faced with nervousness, anger and worst of all fear when playing golf. When first learning the process some say that it is difficult to commit to seeing a positive future. They allow the negative emotions to overwhelm them. Even after successful use of the process fear can get in the way.

Fear is a powerful adversary because it doesn't play fairly, it sneaks up when we least expect it. Mentors have shared with us what Fear really stands for False Evidence Appearing Real or Forget Everything and Run. When battling fear we must remember the words of the Chinese Philosopher Tsun Tsu, "Every battle is won before it is fought." By committing to the process the battle is already won.

At the first sign of discomfort, whether it is nervousness, anger, fear, or any other negative emotion simply **STOP**! Replace the negative input with positive input. The **STOP technique** has been used by psychologists and personal development coaches for many years as a way to facilitate personal development. Doran Andry and Joseph

McClendon, describe its use on a daily basis for personal development.

Because golf is a metaphor of life and especially due to the time between shots in golf the technique is perfectly suited to *"Keep it REAL."*

At the first sign of discomfort *"S"* say it **STOP**! Recognizing the negative thoughts and saying Stop breaks up the negative visual, verbal and kinesthetic inputs. If someone yelled FORE as you were preparing for your shot, you would stop and take cover. This changed the information you were processing from the shot you were playing to protecting yourself. Saying **STOP** breaks the pattern and creates a schetoma, which is a vacuum of emotions. This is a lot like the situation when my wife is angry and letting me know why and the phone rings. After she answers and talks to her mother, she often forgets why she was angry to begin with. The pattern has been broken.

After breaking the pattern *"T"* take a deep breath. This will create a kinesthetic change by adding oxygen to your system; this will actually widen the vacuum of emotions that you have created.

Now the fun part! Fill the vacuum with a predetermined positive outcome *"O"*. The positive outcome we are focusing on is the *REAL Golf Process*. Allow yourself to begin the process all over again. The best players in the world find themselves out of their process. You can see PGA Tour players choose a club and then put it back in the bag if they are distracted and then begin the process over by taking out the same club and starting over. By playing your round as a series of ten second events, you can start the process over at any time.

"P" Praise yourself for returning to the process. Use a positive verbal and kinesthetic trigger to reinforce your praise. Again, it can be as simple as closing your fist and saying, "Yes." You decide what you are comfortable with. Praise has proven to be the best motivator in life, whether it is personally, professionally, or athletically. Recognizing your success and praising yourself replaces the fear and any other negative emotions.

It is ok to go through this process several times during a round if necessary. The dynamic completely changes if a player praises themselves if they got out of their process, STOPPed and then returned to the process. Praising yourself for returning to the process reinforces the process itself. Reward yourself for a good shot! Repetition is the mother of skill. Reward is the father of success.

"STOP"

"S"- Say it...STOP

"T"- Take a Deep Breath

"O"- Focus on the Outcome
The REAL Golf Process

"P"- Praise yourself for
returning to
The REAL Golf Process

Evaluating your Round
Ch. 5

In this Chapter
- ➢ **Evaluating Your Round**
- ➢ **Post Round Checklist**
- ➢ **Exercises**
    - ⇒ **REAL Scorecard**

Evaluate each round ***after*** the round is complete. Many players begin evaluating their round after the fifth hole, or at the turn after the ninth hole. Ask many players "how is it going?" at the end of the front nine and they will tell you every thing they have done wrong thus far and why. They are trying to evaluate the round before it is done. This would be like asking a chef how good the meal was after serving the appetizers. If a player has gone into evaluation mode, there is no way that they can be completing the *REAL Golf Process* for each shot. There is plenty of time to evaluate your round when you have finished.

Begin your evaluation of your round by examining how well you used your process. Ask yourself, "What did I do well today?" Reward yourself for the good shots (or shot) that you made. Look at the positive aspects of the round first!

After you have rewarded yourself, and only after you have taken the time to savor the good shots, ask yourself "what do I need to work on to improve?" How you answer this question is very important. It will be the basis to formulate a practice plan that will lead to improvement. Typically there are two areas to examine, mechanical errors and evaluation errors.

Every shot will not be "perfect"; the key is managing your misses. We say that in every round to that it is OK to hit some shots that are "ugly but effective." The commercials that had a variety of people saying, "I'm Tiger Woods" were misleading." You are not Tiger Woods, only Tiger is Tiger. You will miss hit some shots, get over it. In fact Tiger even misses shots. The key is keeping the misses within a manageable margin of error. This margin of error will change as you become more experienced.

Did you have mechanical errors? If so, then remember the ball flight direction that was the predominant error. This information feedback will help your coach to serve your needs during your next session. It will also help with your next practice session. If you were hitting short irons well, but struggled with your fairway woods you will be able to focus your session with those clubs. If putting was the below your standards you can spend more time on the putting green. I should point out that typically players do not spend nearly enough time practicing in the short game area. I encourage you to increase your practice time in the short game, chipping and putting. It is amazing how a good chip or putt will erase the swing errors from the memory.

Did you have evaluation errors? Evaluation errors are those that arise when you hit the shot you wanted to hit, but planned incorrectly. This is usually referred to as course management. If you made an error in judging how to play a shot, you can learn and apply the knowledge the next time you have a similar situation. Evaluation errors often come by not allowing for your margin of error. Players try to squeeze shots into places that they have no business trying to go. The most common evaluation errors come after a missed shot. Why would you try to hit a shot through a two foot window between trees? If you were good enough to play that shot, would you be standing in the trees?

If you are unfamiliar with a golf course, evaluation errors are common. Tour players play several practice rounds before tournaments, they hit different shots from different locations and practice putts from many different places on the greens, taking into account the possible pin placements. The majority of the players and their caddies keep copious notes about the courses they play. Most of us do not have this luxury, we learn about the course as we play. The more golf experience we develop the easier it becomes to make accurate evaluations. We simply need time in learning to make accurate evaluations. If you are making a consistent evaluation error, you can change the plan. The most common error is not playing enough club to hit the ball all the way to the hole. If you notice that you are always short of the green, a simple adjustment would be to play an additional club the next time you play. In other words, if you think that the club is 8 iron, hit a smooth 7 iron instead. If you notice that you are missing fairways to the right, tee the ball up on the right side of the tee markers and aim down the left side. This will allow you more room to play the shot.

The key to the evaluation is to reward yourself for what you did well to build upon the success and then focus the practice on positive improvement. We are not focusing on what we did wrong; we are concentrating on creating a plan for success! The plan can be created upon realistic goals and objectives for success instead of error correction.

By first recognizing and rewarding yourself for the strengths of your round you build momentum for your next practice session. You can then use this momentum to work on the portions of the game that can take you to another performance level when they are improved. The key is that you will be approaching your practice from a positive perspective, building to a new level rather than fixing mistakes.

Post Round Checklist

-What did I do well? Reward is the father of success.
- What were my best shots of the day?
-Where do I focus improvement? Mechanics and/or
   Evaluation
-What were my best shots of the day?
(Yes, reward yourself!!)

What did I do well?	
Best shots of the day?	
Mechanical Errors	
Evaluation Errors	
Focus for improvement	
Best shots of the day?	

REAL Golf Scorecard

Many players use scorecards that are specially designed to analyze statistics such as fairways hit, greens in regulation and putting. These are very good tools for measuring your physical performance. The following scorecard has been developed to assist you in developing your *REAL Golf Process*. It can be used at any golf course that you play, along with the other types of scorecards or without them. Make copies of the page and keep them in you bag so you always have them at your disposal. When first using the scorecard it is recommended that you use it individually. Focus on your *REAL Golf Process* first, once comfortable with the use of the REAL scorecard, it is easy to incorporate both cards.

There is a place on the scorecard to keep your stroke score. There is also a place to keep track of how many strokes you were committed to and used the *REAL Golf Process*. Use the process scorecard by recording how well you executed all four steps of the process through the hole. To determine your REAL score, begin with your stroke score and then subtract the number of strokes executed with the *REAL Golf Process*. An example of a REAL scorecard is included. As you can see on hole # 3 the player made 5 but was only in the process 3 of the shots, the REAL Score on the hole is 2. On hole #10 the player made 4 on the par 5 hole and committed to and executed all 4 in the *REAL Golf Process*, the REAL score is 0. Zero is the number used to describe scratch golfers. Our ultimate goal is an 18 hole score of zero. Make copies of the card to use each round.

Hole	Par	Score	Process	REAL Score
1	5	5	5	0
2	4	4	4	0
3	4	**5**	3	**2**
4	3	3	3	0
5	4	4	4	0
6	3	4	3	1
7	4	4	4	0
8	4	4	4	0
9	5	5	4	1
Out	36	38	34	**4**
10	**5**	**4**	**4**	**0**
11	4	4	4	0
12	4	4	4	0
13	3	4	3	1
14	4	4	4	0
15	3	3	2	0
16	4	4	4	0
17	4	5	4	1
18	5	4	4	0
In	36	36	33	2
Total	72	74	67	**6**

As you use the card, you will be able to see that the *REAL Golf Process* has a positive impact on your stroke score. Stay consistent with your record keeping and watch the improvement. When asked what your handicap is, you will be able to smile and tell them that you are a REAL scratch-golfer, and they will know you are "A REAL Player".

Scorecard

Hole	Par	Score	Process	REAL Score
1				
2				
3				
4				
5				
6				
7				
8				
9				
Out				
10				
11				
12				
13				
14				
15				
16				
17				
18				
In				
Total				

Practice makes perfect, except in golf.
Practice makes better.
CH. 6

In this Chapter
- ➤ <u>Peaks and Valleys</u>
- ➤ <u>Creating Good Habits</u>
- ➤ <u>Simulated Rounds</u>

Peaks and Valleys

In life we go through peaks and valleys, golf performance also has ups and downs. One of the beautiful things about golf is that we can never master it. We are hitting a ball with a crooked stick in a myriad of conditions. What we can do is create situations that allow us to perform at our best.

While sitting in a chair at my parents ranch in the plains of Oklahoma a cloud came up and here came the rain. For about a half hour it rained really hard. Then as quickly as they had come, the clouds passed through and the sun began to shine. My Mom walked outside and said to my daughters, "You see girls, you appreciate the sunshine after a good cloud of rain." To appreciate growth we must work patiently through some dark clouds. As we work on our *REAL* Golf Process, We must allow changes to happen, and changes take time. My Mom also pointed out another valuable lesson to my daughters at the ranch; the animals will roost when they are ready, not before. You cannot force things to happen, you must create situations that will allow them to happen. There is no firm time table for REAL learning, we all process change in our own unique way. The key, as my mentors have taught me, is to remember that "for things to change, we must be willing to change."

Golf is a series of complex movements that are made sequentially in a variety of circumstances. It is sometimes difficult to make changes. As in life players find comfort in doing things a certain way. Many people drive to work using the exact same route for years. They never deviate from their routine, even if alternative routes could be easier and faster. Very few players begin with a blank slate. People do not typically go directly to a golf instructor with new clubs and zero knowledge. I have given lessons to couples and had the wife tell me they had never touched a club before. The husband tells me that he plays, and just wants a couple of "tips". In a short period of time the wife is beating the husband. This is because she knows only good habits. He has muscle memory that has to be replaced with new memory. Golfers do pick up bad habits. The challenge is to **eliminate bad habits by creating good ones**. Here we go again, simple but not easy.

The reason that golfers do not take the time to create good habits is because the golf learning does not happen in an immediate linear fashion. Very seldom does a person make a change that immediately causes improvement. Our society has become one that expects immediate results. Cell phone calls, text messaging, email all allow us to process information so much faster that we expect results to occur immediately. I know that I am showing my age, but I remember a time that if someone left a phone message and I called them back within a couple of days they were glad to hear from me. If you leave a voicemail on someone's cell phone, how fast are you expecting them to return the call?

Usually a person has to take time to process the changes. I have had many people give me the dog look, the tilt of the head with the eyes almost crossed, during a session when they hit a ball sideways and I tell them, "Yes, that is what I want to see!" They have begun to create a good change, even though the immediate results of the ball flight did not show it. With time and practice you will develop good habits that send the bad habit into extinction. Allow yourself time to create the good habit.

The second most frustrating part of the game of golf is that standards of performance change very quickly. Many times what would have been considered a great shot several months earlier is considered a poor shot by players. Instead of focusing on the improvement in performance people zoom in on the mistakes that they make. When learning new habits, shots may not feel as solid as they did the day  before. If a person scrubs the changes and reverts back to the old motions, they will limit their growth.

Understand that your standards will change. Typically they change faster than the time it takes to create new habits. As golfers we often have to enjoy success in perceived failure. Do not expect non-golfers to understand this, it is part of the golf addiction. If a player didn't score as well as they wanted to, but they focused on their process and good habits on every shot, it has been a successful day.

Committed *REAL players* Brian and John have well surpassed their scoring goals. In evaluating recent rounds we have been able to have a laugh about rounds that they were dissatisfied with even though the score was well beyond their original goals. Both smiled and said, "...ready to take it to a new level Coach!" Of course I replied, "Let's Go!"

I love the point of golf development when I can work with a player about a part of their golf swing that they were unable to work on before. In a session with Schmitty recently he told me that he was ready to go to the next level, he had never hit the ball as well as he was. I had to ask him, are you willing to go through the next learning valley? A learning valley comes from the necessary time that it takes to make changes. It often takes a step backward to take two steps forward. It is a question that needs to be thought out carefully. If you have an important round of golf coming up, that is not the time to begin to make changes. That is the time to reinforce what you are currently doing. If you are happy with you performance level it is ok to continue to reinforce the process you are working on.

It is important to set realistic goals and objectives with golf. If you are going to practice four times a year and play six times is it realistic to think that you are going to score under par? Set realistic goals for yourself and your enjoyment of the game will be much higher. Measure your success based upon what you, do not what others do. Golf is about you and the golf course. You cannot control what your opponent does. Jack Nicklaus, the greatest major champion in golf history won 20 major championships, but came in second 58 times. Fifty-eight times he came close but did not win, failure? I would say that is amazing success.

Creating good habits with good practice

In a recent session, Nobie a *REAL player* who had a hole-in-one after her first few months of sessions, expressed her happiness in the way that she had played in a round. "I haven't even been practicing with my driver," she said. Due to a wrist injury, she had focused her practice on the *REAL Golf Process*, especially with her short game and short irons. She was able to perform through concentrated practice on her *process*.

First and foremost remember that the object of the game is to get the ball into the hole. Having the greatest driving range swing in the world does not equate to being a *REAL player*. Begin your practice close to the hole and work your way back from the hole. A six inch putt counts the same on the scorecard as a 300 yard drive. According to the PGA, shots of 50 yards or less make up at least 60% of the average player's strokes, yet people spend far less time practicing that portion of the game. Take the time to practice your *REAL Golf Process* with these shots. Regardless of your experience, most people can hit the ball 50 yards.

Chipping and pitching are the paramedics of golf. This portion of the game can take you from the metaphorical verge of death and bring you back to life. It is impossible to

practice the *REAL Golf Process* in this area too much. Short game proficiency will take you to lowers scores very quickly.

Only after the short game practice is complete should players work on their golf swing. Yet the typical player goes to the practice center, beats 100 golf balls and believes that they practiced playing golf. Often times beginning the session with the driver trying to see how far they can hit it. *REAL* players practice their *REAL Golf Process*, every shot of their practice sessions. You can be far more efficient hitting 50 shots with your process than, beating 200 golf balls.

PGA Tour players spend four to five hours playing practice rounds at the courses they compete. They hit different shots from various places on the course and putt to different targets on the greens. This allows them to work on their process, under a variety of circumstances. The score of the round is not important. Most people do not have this luxury. Due to family, job and other time restrictions the only opportunity to go to the golf course is for an hour to an hour and a half of practice. The opportunities to take the time necessary to play a round of golf are limited, and when playing you want the most enjoyment possible out of the round. *REAL* players practice efficiently, preparing for the next round of golf.

REAL Practice can help you become a *REAL* player. Ask Annette, who began her golf experience by asking, "This is how I hold it?" She had never touched a club before. Now through her efforts and her ever evolving process she enjoys golf in ways she never imagined.

Simulated Round

A proven method of preparation for a round that can be done in a limited time span is a simulated round. After practicing putting and chipping it is possible to play a simulated round of golf on the practice tee. By playing a simulated round of golf one can practice the *REAL Golf Process* with each shot that they play. This will reduce anxiety, raise confidence, improve performance and most of all make your practice sessions more fun.

To play a simulated round the first step is to choose your favorite golf course or one that you play often. Use the scorecard or yardage book from the course as a guide for your round. Hit some shots to warm up. Remember to hit every shot at a target, always practice to a target. Play REAL golf on the course by visualizing each shot on the practice tee. Go through each step of the process for every shot that you play. Pick various targets to simulate the yardages that would be encountered during the round.

There are several benefits of playing a simulated round. First and foremost is that you are practicing the process that you will use on the course. The repetition of using the process will reinforce using your process during your REAL round of golf. By evaluating and committing to shots and then letting them go the practice session will prepare you for the actual shots that you will play. This will also improve your visual, verbal and kinesthetic input when facing these shots on the course. The simulated round allows you to play a shot a second time if you make a mechanical error. You can take mulligans during your simulated so you don't need them during your REAL round. The greatest advantage is that this can be done in a short time period. Nine holes of a simulated round can be played in less than one hour. Students of all ability levels enjoy the practice sessions playing simulated rounds. When faced with limited time, you don't have to limit your REAL practice. You have had the opportunity to play your practice round prior to playing your REAL round of golf.

Closing Thoughts from the Coaches

Congratulations on beginning your journey to become a *REAL player.* Your commitment to your process will allow you to play golf to your ultimate potential. Feel free to read and complete the exercises more than once. We re-read this book before every tournament and speaking engagement to reinforce our commitment to the process. The more you use the process the more comfortable you will feel with using it.

Regardless of your current playing ability or level of experience the *REAL Golf Process* will help you enjoy golf and improve your performance. Staying with the *REAL Golf Process* will help keep your mind and body in sync. The positive energy that you create allows the body and mind to work together as one.

You will find that you will enjoy golf more because you will be playing better. You will be playing better because you have committed to the *REAL Golf Process.*

We wish you great success and lots of fun playing the wonderful game of golf.

Fairways and Greens.
Keep it REAL!

Notes

Notes

www.Play*REAL*Golf.com

Visit our website to schedule the following
Play *REAL* Golf services.

- Seminars
- Clinics
- Conferences
- Schools
- Tournaments
- Individual Instruction
- Group Instruction
- Play *REAL* Golf DVD's

Phone consultations regarding Assessment, Goal Setting and the
Play *REAL Golf Process* are available by appointment.

**Order Play REAL Golf books with
Special Personalized Messages.**

Order Play REAL Golf gift packages.

Learn how to play and enjoy *REAL* golf!

Visit us at: www.Play*REAL*Golf.com

LaVergne, TN USA
08 February 2010
172371LV00002BA/4/A

9 781598 582284